The Sweetest Swing in Baseball

By
REBECCA GILMAN

D1157839

Dramatic Publishing
Woodstock, Illinois • England • Australia • New Zealand

*** NOTICE ***

IMPORTANT BILLING AND CREDIT REQUIREMENTS

All producers of the Play *must* give credit to the Author of the Play in all programs distributed in connection with performances of the Play and in all instances in which the title of the Play appears for purposes of advertising, publicizing or otherwise exploiting the Play and/or a production. The name of the Author *must* also appear on a separate line, on which no other name appears, immediately following the title, and *must* appear in size of type not less than fifty percent the size of the title type. Biographical information on the Author, if included in the playbook, may be used in all programs. *In all programs this notice must appear:*

Produced by special arrangement with
THE DRAMATIC PUBLISHING COMPANY of Woodstock, Illinois

In addition, all producers of the Play must include the following acknowledgment on the title page of all programs distributed in connection with performances of the Play and on all advertising and promotional materials:

"*The Sweetest Swing in Baseball* was first presented by
the Royal Court Theatre, London."

The Sweetest Swing in Baseball was originally produced by The Royal Court Theatre, London, in March 2004.

CAST:

Dana	Gillian Anderson
Roy/Gary	John Sharian
Erica/Dr. Stanton	Kate Harper
Brian/Michael	Demetri Goritsas
Rhonda/Dr. Gilbert	Nancy Crane

Director:	Ian Rickson
Designer:	Hildegard Bechtler
Lighting Designer:	Howard Harrison
Sound Designer:	Ian Dickinson
Composer:	Peter Salem
Assistant Director:	Maria Aberg
Stage Manager:	Tariq Rifaat
Deputy Stage Manager:	Leila Jones
Assistant Stage Manager:	Hannah Ashwell Dickinson

THE SWEETEST SWING
IN BASEBALL

A Play in Two Acts
For 2m., 3w., with doubling

CHARACTERS:

PLACE: A gallery and a mental hospital in and near a large city.

TIME: The present.

NOTES: When Dana is being Darryl, she doesn't imitate him or try to talk like an African-American. Her language and physicality may be a little bit looser, but she is essentially herself.

The character of Gary should not be played as a psycho à la Hannibal Lector or any other "psycho" types. He is more of a hard-boiled crank.

5

Sets and costumes should be very minimal. Dana can wear the same costume for the entire play (black slacks and a white T-shirt, for example) and it can be dressed up or down with accessories. She can make her changes on stage as the scenery changes around her.

THE SWEETEST SWING IN BASEBALL

SCENE ONE

In a back room of a gallery. DANA stands. She wears a nice shirt over a T-shirt, a pair of black pants and a pair of sandals. The sounds of an opening—people talking, laughing—from the room behind her. She is drinking white wine from a plastic cup.

ROY enters, carrying two more cups of wine. He is wearing a tailored leather coat and a black porkpie hat. He has been looking for her.

DANA. More wine?

ROY. You want it?

DANA. Yeah. *(Takes the wine.)*

ROY. Do you want to go out front?

DANA. I just want to stay back here for a while, okay?

ROY. Okay. *(She downs the rest of her cup, puts the full cup in the empty one.)* It's going great.

DANA. Uh-huh.

ROY. I think they've all dried. There's a lot of hot air in the room. *(She doesn't respond.)* Scott's here. And Maria. And Peter and Phoebe.

DANA. Is that Stacey woman here?

ROY. Yeah. They want to go get a beer.

DANA. So go.

ROY. With you.

DANA. I can't leave my own show.

ROY. Then, do you want to go out front?

DANA. Have I sold anything?

ROY. I don't know.

(ERICA, an assistant at the gallery, enters.)

ERICA. Here you are. How long have you been back here?

DANA. An hour. Roy says nothing's sold.

ERICA. People are more cautious. With the economy.

DANA. Right.

ERICA. The paintings are great. They remind me of when I was a kid? In Utah? At night the color of the desert was that sort of purple black. But you had to look to really see it. To see that it wasn't just black. They're beautiful.

DANA. Can you tell they're still wet?

ROY. They're not all wet.

DANA. I kept seeing things that needed fixing. But maybe I should have left them alone.

ERICA. The shading's so subtle.

DANA. Maybe they're better than I think.

(RHONDA, the gallery owner, joins them.)

DANA. How's it going?

RHONDA. Good good.

ERICA. It's going great.

ROY. Rhonda.

RHONDA. Roy.

ROY *(to DANA)*. You want some more wine?

DANA *(looks at her full cup)*. Yes.

ROY. I'll get it. *(He exits.)*

RHONDA. Listen Dana, whatever happens, I want you to know I'm really proud we're showing your work. We all feel that way.

ERICA. We do.

RHONDA. Whether the critics like it or not or whether anything sells, isn't important. What's important is that the gallery is proud of the work we show. *(Small beat.)*

DANA. It's totally bombing, isn't it?

RHONDA. No.

DANA. The show sucks. Everybody hates it.

ERICA. I love them.

DANA. You have to love them, you're my dealer.

ERICA *(nervous laugh)*. Rhonda's your dealer.

RHONDA. When Erica has her own gallery, she can be your dealer.

DANA. I wasn't saying…

ERICA *(laughs)*. It's not a plan or anything. *(Beat.)*

RHONDA. Dana, it's complicated work.

ERICA. People will have to wait for the critics to explain it. Then they'll love it.

DANA. Who's here?

RHONDA. Carl Jaffe.

DANA. God.

ERICA. Now, your last show, you thought you got such a bad review from him and then I had fifteen people congratulate me on that review.

DANA. He did not say a single positive thing about my work.

ERICA. He was very respectful.

DANA. He called me opportunistic and evacuated. *(Small beat.)*

RHONDA. Rachel Taylor is here.

ERICA. Oh, she's been very supportive.

DANA. Of other people.

RHONDA. You know, if you do work that's less accessible, you're not going to get the sort of unqualified response you've had in the past. Which is a choice you've made, isn't it?

DANA. I guess.

RHONDA. You're making everybody nervous though, standing back here. You should talk to people. *(She exits.)*

DANA. Why would I choose to be inaccessible?

ERICA. Shit just flows from her mouth.

DANA. She wants you to steal me away so she won't have to deal with me.

ERICA. That's not true.

DANA. I don't think she wants to include me in the biennial.

ERICA *(worried)*. Why do you say that?

DANA. She already said something about not having the space to have as many artists…

ERICA. She did?

DANA. She'd want something new. They always want something new.

ERICA. So do something new.

DANA. I don't have any ideas. I pulled these out of my ass.

ERICA. You did not.

DANA. I don't even know if they're ready to show. *(Small beat. Hard for her.)* I don't know if I'm proud of them. *(ERICA doesn't answer. Beat.)*

ERICA. Roy looks good.

DANA. He's going to leave me.

ERICA. What?

DANA. I think he's cheating on me. Can you see—he keeps talking to that Stacey Edwards woman.

ERICA. Who's Stacey Edwards.

DANA. She's this woman who was in a Smiths video in like, 1985. Nobody can get over it.

ERICA. Roy's not cheating on you.

DANA. He wants to.

ERICA *(deep breath)*. How are things going with your new therapist?

DANA. I stopped seeing her.

ERICA. Why?

DANA. She didn't believe anything I told her. Just factual things, like how my dad died. I said he died of pneumonia and she said, "Pneumonia?" I was like, "Yeah, people die of pneumonia. I can get you the death certificate if you don't believe me."

ERICA. Do you think you could find somebody else?

DANA. I had somebody else. I had Dr. Russell but she died.

ERICA. I know.

DANA. I loved her. She didn't just tell me how special I was. She tried to help me figure out ways to fix things. These other people are clueless. I'm on my fifth one already.

ERICA. Maybe you're too picky.

DANA. Dr. Rosenberg fell asleep while I was talking to her.

ERICA. Well, we have to find someone because I'm worried about you. *(Hates to say it.)* I do think your work is suffering.

DANA *(stifling the yell)*. Oh my God, you don't think I know that?!

(ERICA reaches out to take her hand when BRIAN enters. He is very hip.)

BRIAN. Hey. Congratulations.

DANA *(quickly composing herself)*. Hi, Brian. Thanks for coming.

ERICA *(to DANA)*. I'll get you some more wine. *(ERICA exits.)*

BRIAN *(indicates the front room and the paintings)*. They're really intriguing.

DANA. Thanks.

BRIAN. I thought I read in some interview, though, that you were going to show that series on iconic portraiture.

DANA. I don't think I called it "iconic portraiture." It was more just…portraits.

BRIAN. Did you change your mind?

DANA. I didn't finish them. And I was committed to these dates so I did these instead.

BRIAN. Well these are really intriguing.

DANA. Thanks. *(Beat. Trying to be nice.)* So what's going on with you?

BRIAN. Well. I just got this intermedia arts grant for an installation I'm doing at CAM in March.

DANA. Congratulations.

BRIAN. And then I've got a show at Riley Kuhn. In December.

DANA. No way! That's great.

BRIAN. I'm really pleased.

DANA. You should be. That's a huge deal.

BRIAN. Yeah. I really wanted it. *(Small beat.)* I guess I should thank you for recommending me. Bill Riley said you sent him over to Presence, to see my stuff in that loan show.

DANA. Oh, it was my pleasure. I thought it was really good work.

BRIAN. Yeah, he totally dug it.

DANA. Good. *(Beat.)* So you're welcome.

BRIAN. Right, thanks. *(They drink their wine.)* So what's next for you?

DANA. I don't have anything lined up right now.

BRIAN. You'll be in the biennial though.

DANA. Should be, yeah.

BRIAN. Well I can't wait to see those portraits. Let me know when they're finished.

DANA. I will.

BRIAN. And come see my show.

DANA. I will.

(He exits. DANA stands alone for a moment. ROY enters with another cup of wine.)

ROY. What did the Boy Wonder want?

DANA. You're going to leave me, aren't you?

ROY *(regards her)*. You're really in a bad place tonight.

DANA. What is good? Tell me what's good.

ROY. Why don't we go?

DANA. You promised you'd stay through the show.

ROY. I have.

DANA. And then what? You're going to run off with Stacey Edwards?

ROY. No.

DANA. Then what are you going to do?

ROY. Nothing.

DANA. You're going to run off with Stacey Edwards.

ROY. No I'm not.

DANA. You follow her around like a lost puppy.

ROY. No, Dana, I follow you around like a lost puppy. Is what I do. I fetch your wine. I carry your coat. When people talk to you, I blend into the wainscoting. Okay? *(Pause. DANA regards him.)*

DANA. You haven't worked on your boxes in so long.

ROY. Yeah. Well. Who wants Roy Crenshaw's mixed media when they can have a Dana Fielding instead? *(Beat.)*

DANA. So when are you leaving?

ROY. Sweetie.

DANA. When?

ROY *(in spite of himself)*. Soon. *(Beat.)* You asked me to stay through the summer. And I did. And last spring. I stayed through that too. And the show. But it's October. And I'm just a boyfriend, you know? I'm not a—mental health professional or whatever. And I can joke around and watch you paint, but I can't seem to talk you out of whatever it is you're in. Obviously. I wish I could, but I can't. *(Beat.)*

DANA. Then I think the sooner you go the better.

ROY. Dana—

DANA. It's okay.

ROY. I never would have picked tonight to do this.

DANA. It's okay. I picked it.

(RHONDA enters.)

RHONDA. You're still back here?

ROY. Rhonda. *(To DANA.)* I'll see you at home? *(She nods. He exits.)*

RHONDA. You're lucky to have him.

DANA. So everyone says.

RHONDA. You know the people who get it really do get it.

DANA. Oh yeah?

RHONDA. Only...I don't know. Take this for what it's worth, okay? But I was just talking to Rachel Taylor and she said an interesting thing, which is you're much more technically proficient than you used to be. I mean craft-wise, you're among some of the best out there. But, it's almost funny, it's like what people liked about your earlier work was its messiness, you know? I told her, when I saw some of these paintings in their early stages in your studio, there was a rawness to them, and I think I suggested at the time, that they needed to be explained—

DANA. You did.

RHONDA. And the technical changes were really smart, really smart. But now I'm wondering if maybe I was wrong. Because now I'm missing that visceral quality they had. I wonder if you could go back and capture that.

DANA. Is that a question?

RHONDA. More an observation I guess.

DANA. Because it's too late now.

RHONDA. For the future then.

(ERICA enters with another glass of wine.)

RHONDA *(to ERICA)*. You should come meet Tamara
Young.

ERICA. Go ahead. I'll catch up. *(RHONDA exits. ERICA
hands the wine to DANA.)* What do you want to do?
(DANA shrugs. She might cry.) Do you want to take
some time off?

DANA. I don't know.

ERICA. What if you just took some time off and you spent
some time by yourself, and you stopped listening to
these assholes? *(Beat.)* Dana?

BLACKOUT

SCENE TWO

*The occupational therapy room at a psychiatric hospital.
At a table sit DANA, GARY and MICHAEL. GARY is a
regular-looking man, 40, wearing hospital scrubs and a
pocket T-shirt and slippers. MICHAEL is thin, 28, looks
terrible. His hair is a mess and his hands shake. DANA
is wearing the white T-shirt, black pants and flip flops.
She looks rumpled, her hair pulled back. Each of her
wrists is wrapped in clean white bandages, five inches
wide. GARY is drawing with a charcoal pencil. MI-
CHAEL stares into space, an untouched pencil and paper in front of him. DANA sits in the middle with a pile
of modeling clay which she is simply mashing between
her fingers.*

GARY, who has been working intently on his drawing, glances over at his two companions.

GARY. The name of the game is occupational therapy. *(DANA looks at him.)* You should try making something. *(DANA looks at the clay, then she takes what's in her hand and rolls it into a ball. She puts the ball on the table. She and GARY look at it.)* That's terrific. A ball.

DANA *(looks at it)*. It's a cannonball, actually.

GARY. Suit yourself. But the time goes faster if you make something. *(GARY shows her his drawing.)* Here's what I've been working on.

DANA *(eyes widen)*. Wow.

GARY. I know. The verisimilitude, right?

DANA. Yeah.

GARY *(senses something in the way she's looking at it)*. What?

DANA. Nothing. It's great.

GARY. It's not finished.

DANA. I know.

GARY. This guy's arm is too long.

DANA. It's a little long.

GARY. He looks like a fucking ape. *(GARY pulls the drawing back.)*

DANA. I didn't say that. It's just a little long. *(GARY starts erasing the line, frustrated. DANA hesitates, but then jumps in.)* Have you tried drawing the negative space? Instead of the object itself?

GARY. The what?

DANA. The negative space is the space around the object. *(Indicating on the drawing.)* Like, there's a triangle here, between this guy's arm…and this guy's neck…and the knife blade. That's the negative space, see? There should be more length to the—what is that?—a carving knife?

GARY. Yeah.

DANA. Lengthen that and you'll fix the length of the arm.

GARY. Uh-huh.

DANA. Do you want me to show you?

GARY. Yeah. *(He pushes the paper over and she draws for him. MICHAEL looks.)*

MICHAEL. Why is that guy's shadow all gloopy like that?

GARY. It's not a shadow, it's blood.

MICHAEL. Oh.

DANA. Then make it reflective—is this a lamppost?

GARY. Yeah.

DANA. Then your primary shadow would be here and the light would hit here. Then—well I don't have a blending pencil but you can use your finger to lighten that edge of the blood pool— *(She works. GARY and MICHAEL watch.)*

GARY. You're getting crap all over your bandages.

DANA. What?

GARY. You're turning your bandages black. *(DANA stops, looks at her bandages, now covered in charcoal.)* You still got the stitches in?

DANA. Yeah.

GARY. Did you cut horizontally or vertically?

DANA. Vertically.

GARY. See, I don't get that. You're worried about slicing your tendons? What does it matter? Presumably you're going to be dead, right?

DANA. I was trying to cut along the artery.

GARY. But I bet you're glad you've got your tendons now, right?

DANA. I guess.

GARY. Where'd you do it?

DANA. In my bathroom.

GARY. Who found you?

DANA. My ex-boyfriend.

GARY. You were expecting him to come by?

DANA. No. *(Beat.)* I told everybody I was going out of town. That's why he came over. Because he thought I wouldn't be there.

GARY. I'd use a gun. That way you'd know for sure.

MICHAEL. I'd jump.

DANA. I used an X-ACTO knife. *(Beat.)* They're very precise.

GARY. If you really wanted to die, you'd be dead. You just wanted attention.

DANA. No I didn't, I wanted to die. I would have too, if my ex-boyfriend hadn't come by to get his stupid Nina Simone CDs.

GARY. How long you been here?

DANA. I got here last night.

GARY. Who's your doctor?

DANA. I don't know. Dr. Stanton admitted me but I haven't met her yet.

GARY. It's hard to get in Stanton's unit. You must know somebody.

DANA. I don't know anybody. My dealer arranged it while I was in the hospital.

MICHAEL. Your dealer?

DANA. My art dealer. Erica. *(Small beat.)*

MICHAEL. I'm in rehab. It's my second time.

GARY. You a crack addict?

MICHAEL. I'm an alcoholic.

GARY. For how long?

MICHAEL. Since I was fifteen. My dad's an alcoholic, not in recovery.

GARY. I've never touched alcohol in my life. The day I end up a gutless alcoholic is the day I want somebody to put a bullet in my brain. *(Small beat. MICHAEL sits up.)*

MICHAEL. So are you a psycho, or what?

GARY. Yeah. I tried to kill a guy. *(Both DANA and MICHAEL sit back.)* You may have heard of him. Kevin Bridges.

MICHAEL. Oh my God. You're that guy. Who tried to kill Kevin Bridges.

GARY. Yeah.

MICHAEL. You're that crazy stalker guy. I heard you were in here.

GARY. Yeah.

MICHAEL. Now, let me get this straight. Do you think you're Kevin Bridges?

GARY. No. I just want to kill him.

MICHAEL. Why?

GARY. Because he is the seat of all evil.

DANA. Kevin Bridges is that newscaster, right?

MICHAEL. He's an anchor on CNN.

GARY. He uses his position in the media to disseminate evil.

DANA *(to GARY)*. Shouldn't you be in jail or something?

GARY. I was remanded to the psych ward. I'm insane. *(They look at him.)* I'm on a lot of medication.

MICHAEL. Oh.

GARY. Normally I'm over in the east wing, but if your doc can prove you're no immediate harm to yourself or

others then you get privileges. I get to come in here and
on Sundays I get to swim.

MICHAEL. You get to swim? I don't get to swim.

GARY. Swimming's a privilege. You have to earn it.

DANA *(to GARY)*. So you're not dangerous?

GARY. Only to Kevin Bridges. *(Beat. GARY regards
DANA.)* You don't seem depressed enough. To try to kill
yourself.

DANA. How the hell would you know?

GARY. Back off. It's a compliment. You seem normal.
(They go back to their work.) Yeah, you'll be out of here
by next week.

DANA. Next week?

GARY. Who's your carrier?

DANA. My what?

GARY. Insurance.

DANA. Golden Rule.

GARY. Ten days is all they'll cover.

DANA. Ten days?

MICHAEL. You get twenty-eight for rehab.

GARY. I got life. *(DANA is preoccupied.)* What's the matter? You afraid to go home?

DANA. No.

GARY. Afraid you'll kill yourself?

DANA. No.

GARY. Why are you afraid of it, if it's what you want to
do?

DANA *(snaps)*. I'm not afraid. Okay?

MICHAEL. Leave her alone.

GARY. Okay. *(DANA picks up a piece of clay and slowly rolls it into a ball.)* So why'd you do it?

BLACKOUT

SCENE THREE

The hospital cafeteria. DANA puts a tray on the table. On it, are a covered plate of breakfast food, a cup of coffee and three glasses with paper spill-guards on top of each. In the glasses are milk, orange juice, and to-mato juice. DR. GILBERT enters. She wears an I.D. badge and carries some files.

GILBERT. Dana?

DANA. Yes.

GILBERT. I'm Nancy Gilbert. I wanted to welcome you to the unit. I'm sorry nobody was here to meet you when you got in, but we usually don't admit patients over the weekends.

DANA. That's okay.

GILBERT. It looks like you're settling in though. I under-stand you've already met Gary Richards.

DANA. He's the psycho?

GILBERT. As long as he's on medication he's stable. But I'd give him a wide berth anyway. Technically, he is a sociopath.

DANA. He did seem kind of cranky.

GILBERT. I'll let you get back to your lunch.

DANA. Yeah. I didn't know—when you fill out your card for what you want, I didn't know you could circle as many things as you wanted. In each category. I thought I could only get coffee. But then I saw people had coffee and juice and then they said I could have as many drinks as I want.

GILBERT *(looks at her tray).* You must be thirsty.

DANA. No. But I only get tomato juice on planes. And then I saw the milk, and that looked good. And then I thought, why not orange juice too? *(Laughs.)* This has been the biggest decision of my day.

GILBERT. Okay then. I'm glad to see you're doing so well.

DANA. Yeah. So do you know when I'm going to see Dr. Stanton?

GILBERT. You'll actually be seeing me for therapy. Dr. Stanton has a full load.

DANA. You're my doctor?

GILBERT. Yes.

DANA. Then forget what I said. I'm not doing well at all.

GILBERT. No?

DANA. I'm doing really crappy.

GILBERT. I see. How are you feeling…crappy?

DANA. Panicky. Then depressed. Then panicky again.

GILBERT *(opens her file).* Were you on any medication? Before your suicide attempt?

DANA. No. I've never taken any.

GILBERT. Why's that?

DANA. I've always been afraid it would mess with my painting. I'm an artist.

GILBERT. I know.

DANA. I thought about taking it, but I looked at my life and I thought—that's why you're depressed. Medication's not going to fix that.

GILBERT. Things didn't look so hot, huh?

DANA. No. I mean, my parents are dead. My boyfriend dumped me —

GILBERT. Back up. When did your parents die?

DANA. My dad died when I was twenty-one. Of pneumonia. *(She gives a small beat to see how this registers. GILBERT nods.)* And my mom died five years ago from cancer.

GILBERT. Is that when you started seeing Dr. Russell?

DANA. How'd you know about Dr. Russell?

GILBERT. She and Dr. Stanton shared a practice. That's how you got here. The unit was full, but Dr. Stanton made an exception.

DANA. That's so nice. I thought maybe Erica bribed you or something, to get me off her hands. I mean, I haven't even heard from her in over a month. But that's what happens, you know. Your career's in the toilet and everybody treats you like you're a leper. Like failure's contagious. Get it off me! Get it off me! Everybody stopped calling me. Silence. *(Beat. GILBERT watches her.)* Like that.

GILBERT. I'm only trying to catch up. Didn't your friend Erica say you had a big opening?

DANA. At Rhonda Block. Yes. It was a huge deal. It tanked.

GILBERT. What?

DANA. It completely tanked. I got creamed in the press and I didn't sell crap and it was a train wreck.

GILBERT. But this was only one show.

DANA. It's been a steady decline. My first show, everybody was all hyped up. They were all saying I was like, the new vision of a new generation or something, but with every show since then everybody's been acting like

I'm never going to live up to that original potential. *(Small beat.)* I tried to stop worrying about it. I stopped reading any reviews, because they were completely fucking with my head. Like a while back, this woman Margarite Mosely said I relied too heavily on reds, I had a preponderance of reds in my canvases and so the next time I went to paint, all of a sudden I had a color wheel in my head and it was like the entire spectrum was suddenly off limits. You know? Then I'd put down a yellow and it started looking too orange or the blues were too violet and I got all freaked out and everything just turned out black. Because this one idiot didn't like my reds.

GILBERT. And you're afraid if you go on medication, it might change all this. *(Beat.)*

DANA. Was that a joke?

GILBERT. No. I'm simply clarifying your earlier position. *(Beat.)*

DANA. You're going to kick me out, aren't you?

GILBERT. What?

DANA. I heard my insurance will only pay for ten days.

GILBERT. It depends on your progress—

DANA. I'm self-employed, my insurance is the cheapest one. Golden Rule. I think it only covers if I get hit by a bus.

GILBERT. Then we'll continue therapy on an out-patient basis. We're here to help you for as long as you need help.

DANA. But it'd go a lot faster if I went on the drugs.

GILBERT. I'm not implying that.

DANA. You know, the thing about those stupid drugs is if I take them, that makes me the problem. But I'm not the problem.

GILBERT. It was only a suggestion—

DANA. I'm not trying to kill anybody or hurt anybody. All I'm trying to do is paint. *(Beat.)*

GILBERT. All right. It looks like we have a lot to work on—

DANA *(looks at her tray)*. They told me not to fill out a card for dinner because it's Mexican night. What's Mexican night?

GILBERT. They let our unit use the staff kitchen. You get to make tacos.

DANA. Really?

GILBERT. I understand it's a lot of fun.

DANA. I love tacos.

GILBERT. Okay then, Dana. It's very nice to meet you. *(DANA doesn't answer. She is staring at her tray.)* I'll check on your insurance. Try not to worry, okay? *(DANA looks up.)*

DANA. Just because I love tacos doesn't mean I'm happy. I'm not happy.

GILBERT. I know.

END OF SCENE

SCENE FOUR

The common room. Uncomfortable chairs. MICHAEL and DANA are watching TV. MICHAEL looks more alert, less shaky. DANA has a book in her hand that she is not reading.

MICHAEL. Okay... *(He watches.)* That's the guy I like.

DANA. What does the winner get?

MICHAEL. A recording contract.

DANA. How do they pick?

MICHAEL. You call in and vote. *(They watch. A commercial comes on and MICHAEL mutes it. DANA looks at her book.)*

DANA. The nurse loaned me this romance novel but it's awful.

MICHAEL. We've got a whole library over in rehab. But it's all twelve-step books. Or books by recovering addicts. *(Laughs.)* Half of them, you look at them and the people who wrote the book ended up dead from an overdose.

DANA. This is your second time here?

MICHAEL. Yeah.

DANA. Did something happen...?

MICHAEL. I went on a binge. I mean nothing happened to make me go on a binge, I just went on a binge. And I wasn't eating and my sodium levels went haywire. My super found me in the lobby, I guess I was falling all over the place and I couldn't talk. He thought I had a brain tumor. But. No such luck.

DANA. Don't say that.

MICHAEL. I'm not complaining. I'm alive. They're even holding my job for me.

DANA. What do you do?

MICHAEL. I write code. For computers.

DANA. So you have an actual skill.

MICHAEL *(laughs)*. Yeah.

(ERICA enters. She looks very nervous. She carries a small bag.)

ERICA. Dana?

DANA. Oh, wow.

ERICA. Hey.

DANA. I forgot you were coming.

ERICA. They said you gave permission.

DANA. Yeah, I just— *(She looks at her wrist. She's not wearing a watch.)* I don't have a watch or anything. Is it Tuesday already?

ERICA. It's Wednesday.

DANA *(looks around)*. Did they say where we should go?

MICHAEL. I'll leave.

DANA. You're watching your show.

MICHAEL. I don't mind.

DANA *(to ERICA)*. This is my friend Michael.

MICHAEL. Hi. *(To DANA.)* Come get me when you're through, okay? *(He exits.)*

ERICA *(doesn't know where to start. Hands DANA the bag)*. This is stupid but I brought you make-up.

DANA. Make-up?

ERICA. I called and asked if I could bring anything, and they said a lot of women liked make-up. If you hadn't brought any in with you. When I packed your bag before, I didn't think to put any in. And I...the bathroom was kind of...I only packed your clothes.

DANA. That's okay.

ERICA. It's not much. I know you're more of a "natural look" kind of person. *(Beat.)* Roy wanted to know if he could come.

DANA. No.

ERICA. He feels like you meant for him to find you.

DANA. I didn't mean for anybody to find me.

ERICA. I know. *(Upset.)* You really really scared me.

DANA. I'm sorry.

ERICA. I thought you were going to die. When I got to the hospital Roy was—your blood was on him and I thought you were dead.

DANA. Why was my blood on him?

ERICA. He must have been holding you. *(Beat.)* We both...we felt terrible we didn't call you. I didn't call you for so long because I thought you wanted to be left alone. I thought I would leave you alone but I shouldn't have done that. I didn't know what was happening. And you never called me, so I didn't know.

DANA. I didn't think anybody wanted to talk to me.

ERICA. But you can't go and kill yourself without even, you know, calling to see if maybe I could talk you out of it or something. It's not fair. You have to give people a chance to help you.

DANA. I'm sorry.

ERICA. It's okay. You just scared me. *(They sit. Pause.)* A lot of people have called. *(Laughs.)* Rhonda thinks she drove you to it.

DANA. She kind of did.

ERICA. She still wants to work with you.

DANA *(laughs)*. She probably wishes I was dead. Then she could have a retrospective. Double the prices. People really start to appreciate you when you're dead.

ERICA. People really miss you when you're dead. *(Beat.)* So tell me what they have you doing here. Have you seen Dr. Stanton?

DANA. I've been seeing this Dr. Gilbert woman.

ERICA. Do you like her?

DANA. She's okay. *(Beat.)*

ERICA. What else do you do?

DANA. We have occupational therapy. We watch movies.

ERICA. Are you making some friends?

DANA. There's this guy named Gary who's very interesting. He's...very interested in the news. *(Indicates.)* And Michael. I like Michael. He's not in my unit though.

ERICA. Do you have a roommate?

DANA. Her name's Virginia. She never talks.

ERICA. Why doesn't she talk?

DANA. She never talks and she never gets out of bed. I don't know what the deal is. I did ask her last night if she was hot—it was hot in our room—and she kind of grunted. So that seems promising. *(Beat.)* Dr. Gilbert won't say for sure, but I think I can only stay a few more days. Because of my insurance. It's too expensive. It's a thousand dollars a day so I can't stay if the insurance won't pay.

ERICA. I wish I could help—

DANA. I'm not asking you to pay.

ERICA. I could loan you a couple of thousand but—

DANA. I'm not asking you for money, Erica. I know you don't have money. *(Small beat.)* I don't suppose Rhonda would offer? *(ERICA doesn't answer.)*

ERICA. We'll figure something out.

DANA. Dr. Gilbert says she'll see me on an out-patient basis—

ERICA. Good.

DANA *(overlapping)*. But I'm afraid if I go home, if I have to look at my studio with all that crap everywhere—

ERICA. I tried to clean it.

DANA. And that bathroom—

ERICA. You painted on the walls, though. Should I paint over it?

DANA. With those tiles, those little octagonal tiles. They're so hard not to stare at. I kind of got obsessed with them. But not in a good way. *(Laughs.)* There's that crack along the floor where the tiles to the left are slightly higher than the ones on the right? From there, I tried to count all the tiles but the rows are hard to keep straight and after a while, they kind of blurred together and I stopped seeing the grout. Just these octagons, fitting up against all these other octagons. I had this feeling like, if one of the octagons could just get free. If it could just get away from the other octagons everything would be okay, but... *(Laughs again.)* And then I thought, I'm lying on the bathroom floor. I don't know how I got there. *(Beat.)* It's a very cold floor. When you step out of the shower? It's very cold. *(Small beat.)* Virginia and I both have little stations here, in the bathroom, with a mirror and shelves on either side for our stuff. Then the dresser is built in under the mirror. It's maple. Maple is a nice, warm wood I think.

ERICA *(looks at her. Gentle)*. You could put your make-up on one of the shelves.

DANA. I could. *(They sit for a moment.)* Is there anything in that portrait series you think you could sell?

ERICA. I don't know. You don't want to get overexposed, you know. It makes you a target.

DANA. I tried to kill myself. I already feel like a target.

ERICA. I'm just not sure it's the best strategy right now.

DANA. I don't want a strategy. I want to stay here.

ERICA. I'm thinking about your future.

DANA. What future?

ERICA. Your future. Your career.

DANA. I don't care about my career. Would you stop being my dealer for five seconds and just— *(Stops.)* Just sell the goddamn paintings. *(Beat.)*

ERICA *(reluctantly)*. I don't know if I can. A lot of people passed on the last show. *(Beat.)* And I'm not your dealer, I'm your friend. *(Pause. DANA takes this in.)*

DANA. So...you don't want your fifty percent anymore?

END OF SCENE

SCENE FIVE

The occupational therapy room. GARY is still working on his drawing. MICHAEL is flipping through a book and has another pile of books beside him. DANA has a child's box of watercolors and a Styrofoam cup of water and is painting on a piece of butcher paper.

GARY. If you want to stay you have to have a major diagnosis. Depression won't cut it.

DANA. Like what?

GARY. Paranoid schizophrenic. Multiple personality disorder. Manic depressive.

DANA. I thought about trying to kill myself again—

MICHAEL. Dana.

DANA. But how do I do it? My roommate's on a suicide watch—

MICHAEL. You're probably on a suicide watch.

DANA. Whatever. But they won't even let me keep a blow dryer in the room. In case she wants to electrocute herself. I have to dry my hair at the nurses' station.

GARY. You don't need a blow dryer. There's a million ways if you really want to. You could kill yourself with this pencil. Jab it right through your eyeball and into your brain.

MICHAEL. Could we not talk about this?

GARY. But that's just a stop-gap measure.

MICHAEL. Sticking a pencil in your brain?

GARY. Trying to kill yourself. You buy another ten days, maybe. And unfortunately it's a Catch-22 situation. The fact that you want to stay means you like the safety of the place, which means you have a healthy sense of self-preservation, which means you're not really suicidal, which means you're ready to go home.

DANA. Great.

MICHAEL. Maybe it won't be so bad.

DANA. I'm pretty sure it's going to be bad. *(Beat. MICHAEL looks at what she's painting.)*

MICHAEL. That's cool.

DANA. This is a…it's a tern.

GARY. A what?

DANA. A tern? Like a gull, or a duck?

GARY *(looks)*. I thought you were a famous artist.

DANA. I don't normally paint terns. It's actually, well it's kind of stupid, but when I was a kid I drew my own comic strip? And these were the characters. *(Shrugs.)* But it's stupid.

MICHAEL. No it's not. Who are they?

DANA. Well, this is C.T. Contemplative Tern. He's like the mayor of the woodlands. Because he's so thoughtful.

And this is Deluded Dan the Chipmunk Man. He's obese, but he thinks he's pleasantly plump. Then this is the Ghost Bison. He's haunted by visions of his decimated herd. And then this dot over here is a gnat. He just hangs around and says really smart things when nobody's expecting it. *(GARY and MICHAEL look at the comic.)*

GARY. You should call him Erudite Gnat.

DANA. That's kind of a mouthful.

GARY. No more than Contemplative Tern.

MICHAEL. He has a point.

DANA. Okay. Erudite Gnat. *(Beat.)* Anyway. I used to draw little adventures for them. I had completely forgotten about it but the paints reminded me.

MICHAEL. I wish I had known you when I was a kid. The kids I grew up with were complete jarheads. Creativity to them was blowing up a cat with a cherry bomb.

DANA. The kids I grew up with thought I was weird.

GARY. You were.

MICHAEL *(pushing the books forward, blocking off GARY)*. So anyway, I brought you all these books from our library, but I guess you won't need them if you're leaving.

DANA. I can still read a couple.

MICHAEL. I tried to pick good ones. Mary Tyler Moore. Billy Carter.

DANA. Oh dear.

MICHAEL *(picking up another book)*. This one's good. Darryl Strawberry, *Recovering Life*. Get it? *Recovering life?* Two months after he wrote it he got arrested for possession.

GARY. He was a bum.

MICHAEL. He had a hard life.

GARY. What? Somebody paid him ten million dollars to play catch?

MICHAEL. He had a bad childhood. He didn't have any coping skills.

GARY. He didn't run out routine grounders. Is what he didn't do. He was a drunk.

MICHAEL. Alcoholic.

GARY. Call it what you want, it doesn't change anything. When you have talent like that and you waste it...? *(Beat.)* When he was sober, he had a perfect swing. Perfect follow-through. Sweetest swing I ever saw.

MICHAEL. Yeah. *(Beat.)*

GARY. So you a baseball fan?

MICHAEL. Yeah.

GARY. I thought you were gay.

MICHAEL. The two are not mutually exclusive.

GARY. I just never met a gay guy who was into sports. I've met a lot of gay guys who were drunks though.

MICHAEL. Oh yeah? *(He pushes the books over to DANA.)* Anyway. Read what you can.

DANA. Thanks. *(To GARY.)* Could I fake one of those things? Like the paranoid schizophrenia?

GARY. No way you can fake that. You thinking of faking something?

DANA. I thought maybe if I had something more serious, they wouldn't send me home.

GARY. You're not the first one to think that. But it's too hard. These people are professionals.

DANA. Then they should know not to send me home. *(Pause.)*

GARY. You could maybe buy some time with something milder.

MICHAEL. People fake multiple personality disorders.

GARY. MPD's too hard. You could do like a Mark David Chapman maybe. He just thought he was John Lennon. Which is why he had to eliminate John Lennon. Because John Lennon was impersonating him, Mark David Chapman. Who was John Lennon.

MICHAEL. But you don't think you're Kevin Bridges.

GARY. No. I explained that already.

DANA. Did he walk around acting like John Lennon?

GARY. It was sort of an internal thing. But when he bought the gun that he used to kill John Lennon, he signed the receipt "John Lennon."

MICHAEL. So are you trying to kill Kevin Bridges to impress somebody? Like what's-his-head did, with Jody Foster?

GARY. I already told you why I want to kill him.

MICHAEL. But how is he evil, exactly?

GARY. He's just very evil.

MICHAEL. Does he do evil things?

GARY. Yes.

MICHAEL. Like what?

GARY. He comes into my living room every night and talks down to me. Okay?

DANA. Do I have to kill somebody though? Because I really don't want to kill anybody.

GARY. Not necessarily. But it should have a scary edge to it.

MICHAEL. I don't think it needs to be scary.

GARY. It should stand out, though.

MICHAEL *(to DANA)*. Who are you going to be?

DANA. I don't know.

GARY. Don't pick some artist. Like don't suddenly become Picasso or something. That's way too obvious.

DANA. Oh God. There's no way I'd be an artist. *(What she's said hangs in the air for a moment. The other two look at her.)* What? I want to be something good.

END OF SCENE

SCENE SIX

Dr. Gilbert's office. DANA sits across from her.

GILBERT. For the rest of this session, we should focus on what's going to happen when you leave tomorrow.

DANA. Okay.

GILBERT. How long do you think it will take you to find a new place?

DANA. I don't know. But Erica said I could stay with her if I didn't want to go home.

GILBERT. It would be better if you didn't stay with Erica for too long. We want to get you into a normal routine.

DANA. Can I use the routine I have here? Because before I just slept. And ate toast. And went crazy.

GILBERT. It's not a given, that you'll go back to that.

DANA. You're right. I probably won't sleep. Or eat. *(Beat.)*

GILBERT. You know, these are the very kinds of problems that can be treated with medication—

DANA. No.

GILBERT. Disruptions in sleep patterns, loss of appetite...

DANA. No, I can't.

GILBERT. I'm not talking about lifelong meds. If you don't like the way it makes you feel, we'll take you off—

DANA. I can't, okay? I already explained that to you. *(Tiny beat.)* I have to be drug-free. I have to be drug-free because they come in and they test me.

GILBERT. Someone tests you?

DANA. The commissioner's office. They send somebody in.

GILBERT. What?

DANA. Some dude. From the commissioner's office. He comes in and watches you piss in a cup.

GILBERT. What are you talking about?

DANA. I'm not taking any drugs. I'm not taking any chances that it comes up something weird and they won't let me play.

GILBERT. Play what?

DANA. Baseball.

GILBERT. You play baseball?

DANA *(laughs)*. Hell yeah I play baseball. *(Small beat. Not completely sure.)* I'm The Straw.

GILBERT. What?

DANA. Darryl Strawberry? The Straw? *(GILBERT looks at her.)* Are you okay?

GILBERT. Dana, I—

DANA. Who you callin' Dana?

GILBERT. You.

DANA. Nuh-uh.

GILBERT. Yes.

DANA. No way.

GILBERT. Stop doing whatever you're doing.

DANA. I'm just talkin'.

GILBERT. But what are you talking about?

DANA. How they don't trust me. Like…the comish is always askin', "Is he coked up? Is he on the stuff? The crack? The crank? The…stuff?" So I'm not even takin', like a Tylenol 'cause I'm afraid it's a slippery slope. One second you're popping Advil, the next you're shootin' smack. *(Small beat.)* Although technically I'm not a heroin addict. I'm an alcoholic and I snort cocaine. *(Beat.)*

GILBERT. Dana—

DANA. Why do you keep calling me Dana? My name's not Dana.

GILBERT. Dana.

DANA. Dana's a girl's name. You can call me Darryl. Or you can call me The Straw. I prefer The Straw because it's a nickname my fans came up with, because…it describes me. I'm lanky.

GILBERT. Isn't it just a shortened version of your name— *(Remembers herself.)* I mean, stop it. Whatever it is you're doing, it's not going to work. You have to go home.

DANA. You know who I'd like to talk to, who I have not talked to once and who is s'posed to be the best doctor there is, is this Dr. Stanton lady I keep hearing about.

GILBERT. I consult with her daily about your therapy—

DANA. But I've never consulted with the lady.

GILBERT. Because I'm your doctor and even though you won't listen to me when I give you professional advice, I do know what I'm talking about.

DANA. Then you oughta know I can't be on the outside. I'm dope sick. *(Small beat.)* Plus, I get twenty-eight days for rehab.

GILBERT. Fine. Dana. I'll ask Dr. Stanton to come and talk with you—

DANA. That's all I'm askin'—

GILBERT. So she can explain again why you can't stay because this is an issue of normalcy. Because as much as you might like it here, this is not the real world. And eventually, we all have to live in the real world. All of us. Even Darryl Strawberry. *(Beat. She and DANA regard one another.)*

DANA. I hear what you're sayin'.

GILBERT. Good.

DANA. I gotta step up to the plate. And I mean that literally. Not as a metaphor.

GILBERT. You don't have to explain it.

DANA. 'Cause I'm a professional baseball player—

GILBERT. I get it.

DANA. I'm Darryl Strawberry.

BLACKOUT—END OF ACT ONE

ACT TWO

SCENE ONE

Dr. Gilbert's office, an hour later. DR. GILBERT is gone. DR. STANTON is talking to DANA. STANTON is very maternal, kind—a wise and gentle aunt.

STANTON. You know you're not Darryl Strawberry.

DANA *(thinks)*. Now, if you mean by that, who is the real Darryl Strawberry and is he me? Then yeah, you're right. 'Cause the Darryl that gets projected out there, that's not me. That ain't real.

STANTON. You're Dana Fielding.

DANA. Nope.

STANTON. You're Dana Fielding and you're very sad right now and you don't want to go home because it feels very safe here. But we have this ridiculous situation with your insurance company and the hospital has to discharge you.

DANA. Maybe I should call the players' union.

STANTON. I don't think it would help.

DANA. They could arbitrate.

STANTON *(looks at her)*. Are you afraid you'll hurt yourself, if you leave?

DANA. I might...do some drugs. And hurt myself. Like that.

STANTON. What are the chances you might do something? On a scale of one to five.

DANA *(thinks)*. Four and a half?

STANTON. Well, that's better than five. *(Beat.)* This is a radical question, I know, but have you ever considered another line of work?

DANA. Every day.

STANTON. And?

DANA. See, the thing is this: I love what I do. Or I did love what I do. But it got ruined for me. And now I hate it.

STANTON. How did it get ruined?

DANA. Jeez. Like... *(STANTON waits.)* Like when I was a kid, you know... *(Trails off.)* Like if it seemed like things were sad at home—like my daddy, he wasn't good with money, and sometimes my mama would get sad—when I was a little boy? So I would go to the park. Get in a game. And I was really good at it. All the kids wanted me on their team. And sometimes my parents would come watch me play and I could see it made 'em happy and I liked that. *(Small beat.)* But also, I liked the way it made me feel. Like, I felt real confident. Even if I had a couple of strikes on me, it didn't get me down. I'd say to myself, "Shit, just hit the next one." And I would. But even if I didn't, it didn't matter. It wasn't a league or anything. It was just a bunch of kids from the neighborhood, running around, goofing off. *(Small beat.)* But then everybody wants you to get organized and next thing you know, you're in Little League and all the parents are out there, screaming at the coaches and the coaches are yelling at the kids and it's like, high stakes all of a sudden. And then everybody's telling you "turn pro, turn pro." And then, you know, your mama dies of cancer and your daddy's long gone—'cause he ran off into the projects and became a dope addict or something. But the long and short of it is, you hit a home run and win the World Series and there's nobody there to see it. There's this big fat party and everybody's all over you but when the party's over, you go home by yourself. *(Small beat.)* And then everybody's, "What's next? What's next?" And you're like, "I fucking won the World Series," and they're like, "I don't give a shit. What have you done for me lately?" So you become totally focused on producing. Runs. You get up to bat and it's not, "I'll hit the next one." It's, "I better hit the next one or there goes my average." And then it's not fun anymore, it's work. It's ruined.

STANTON. How long have you been playing baseball?

DANA. Since I was eight?

STANTON. Do you think you're making any progress here? Toward loving it again?

DANA. I don't know. I've been…sort of practicing again.

STANTON. Shagging fly balls, that sort of thing?

DANA. Yeah. And maybe…drawing? It's been kind of fun. The occupational therapy room here reminds me of my old art room in high school.

STANTON. Oh yeah?

DANA. Not that I hung out there a lot. I was mostly in the gym.

STANTON. Right.

(GILBERT enters with some sheets printed off the Internet.)

GILBERT. All right, this should do it. *(To DANA.)* What's your lifetime batting average?

DANA. I don't think you can reduce a man to a set of numbers.

GILBERT. Then what position do you play?

DANA. Outfield.

GILBERT. Right field? Left?

DANA. Center. I'm very versatile. *(GILBERT turns to STANTON, as if to say "See?")*

STANTON. It's hardly a textbook case. *(To DANA.)* Darryl, I'm going to contact your insurance company. This will require that I change your diagnosis. But I'll make it clear to them that you simply need to stay for a while longer.

GILBERT. Boy. *(Ignoring her. To DANA.)* Had you packed?

DANA. Uh-uh.

STANTON. Good then. We'll just carry on as before.

DANA *(pleasantly surprised)*. Thanks. *(She starts to leave. Then to GILBERT, indicating the Internet printout.)* Can I have those?

GILBERT. No.

DANA. No sweat. Like I said, I try not to think about that shit. *(Cheerful.)* Catch you on the rebound.

GILBERT. That's basketball.

DANA. Man. Ease up.

END OF SCENE

SCENE TWO

The occupational therapy room. DANA is standing in front of a canvas with a palette and tubes of oil paint, mixing colors. GARY is still working on his drawing.

MICHAEL. Why'd you pick Darryl Strawberry?

DANA. I don't know. I was reading that book you gave me.

GARY. Do you even know anything about baseball?

DANA. A little. But I don't know anything about his career. The book's just him and his wife talking about his family and God and rehab.

MICHAEL. Where is it?

DANA. I threw it away. I didn't want to get caught with it. But I have to do something. Dr. Gilbert was quizzing me, practically. "What's your batting average?"

MICHAEL. Career was, like, two-sixty. Three hundred and something home runs.

DANA. Is that good?

GARY. Yes, Darryl Strawberry. That's good.

DANA. Well I don't know.

GARY. And why are you painting?

DANA. I felt like it.

GARY. But does Darryl Strawberry paint?

DANA. He could. If he wanted.

GARY. I can't believe you're pulling this off.

DANA. Well Dr. Stanton was convinced. Or highly sympathetic. I'm not sure.

GARY. Are they putting you on anti-psychotics?

DANA. No.

GARY. Because technically, they should be putting you on anti-psychotics.

MICHAEL. Maybe I should try it. I don't want to go home.

GARY. See? Next thing you know, everybody's going to be walking around, acting like he's Eleanor Roosevelt.

MICHAEL. During the week it's okay, I work a lot. But the weekends? It's like time stops. I can't go to a bar, I can't go out with my friends. Of course they probably don't even notice I'm not there.

DANA. I'm sure they do.

MICHAEL. Whatever, I don't care. I just make a big pot of soup. It's really fun. *(It's not fun and he does care. To GARY.)* I thought you wanted her to do it.

GARY. There's a difference between doing it, and doing it right. *(To DANA.)* Like right now. You should be Darryl Strawberry right now. You have to be consistent. With everybody. A nurse could walk in here, hear you chatting, and boom! Cover blown. *(Small beat.)* Lifetime on-base percentage.

DANA. What?

GARY. Your on-base percentage. What was it?

DANA. Six?

GARY. In chronological order, list every team you played for.

DANA. Yankees?

GARY. Wrong!

MICHAEL *(to DANA)*. Mets.

GARY. Who'd you sign with next?

DANA. The Yankees?

GARY. No! You're hopeless.

MICHAEL. No she's not. We can coach her. It'll be fun. She'll be our own Eliza Doolittle. *(DANA starts painting.)* It was Mets, Dodgers, Giants then Yankees.

GARY. I think you forgot Betty Ford in there between the Dodgers and the Giants, and the Giants and the Yankees, and the Yankees and the Yankees.

DANA. Was he always messed up?

MICHAEL. No. He was great. He was Rookie of the Year. Won all these batting titles. But then he got all fucked up. And he kept getting busted and going in and out of rehab. *(Shrugs.)* So the commissioner finally kicked him out of baseball completely. *(Small beat.)* But then he did get clean for real. And he went and played for this independent-league team.

GARY. St. Paul Saints.

MICHAEL. Yeah, it's like, the bottom of the bottom. It's not even a farm team. But he wanted to make a comeback. And he did, he was hitting over four hundred— *(GARY laughs)* —it was insane. All was forgiven, you know. The scouts came back and the Yankees signed him again, he was leading the team in home runs. Then in the middle of the playoffs, he got colon cancer and he couldn't play anymore. Then he started doing drugs again and he got busted again. They finally sent him to prison.

DANA. Why was he like that?

MICHAEL. I remember, he went in front of the judge and told the judge he wanted to die. That the only reason he didn't kill himself, was he didn't want to leave his kids without somebody to take care of them.

DANA. So I picked the most depressing baseball player on the planet.

GARY *(looks at the canvas).* Your duck looks like a chicken.

DANA. It is a chicken.

MICHAEL. Why a chicken?

DANA. I grew up on a farm, upstate. We had a lot of chickens.

GARY. And Darryl Strawberry grew up in south-central L.A. The only chicken he ever saw was at KFC.

DANA. Fine. I'll put a do-rag on its head.

MICHAEL. Put a hat on it.

DANA. What?

MICHAEL. Put a baseball cap on it. Then it will be a baseball-playing chicken.

GARY. Put a bat in its beak.

DANA *(looks at the canvas).* Seriously?

GARY. Darryl Strawberry would.

DANA. No he wouldn't.

GARY. How would you know?

DANA *(looks at the canvas).* Fine.

GARY. And put him in the outfield.

MICHAEL. With a bat?

GARY. I'm talking multiple views.

DANA. I don't want to do multiple views. *(Paints.)* Although, with baseball diamonds you get those nice greens.

MICHAEL. And the groundskeeper mows the grass so there are those stripes in it. Dark green then shimmery green. *(GARY gives him a look.)* It's nice.

DANA *(pleased).* Yeah. *(Starts to paint. After a moment, she begins to speak, practicing.)* I remember the first time I walked out onto the field at Shea Stadium. *(Gives*

GARY a "See, I know some things" look.) I'd signed with the Mets straight outta college—

GARY. High school.

DANA. Straight outta high school and I'd never been to the big city before.

MICHAEL. He played in the minors first. Texas League.

DANA. And I'd never seen the great plains of Texas. I didn't have a dime to my name—

GARY. He got two hundred thousand dollars as a signing bonus. It was a huge deal.

DANA. I had two hundred thousand big ones in my pocket. *(Small beat.)* That was a helluva lot of pressure. People asking, "Who is this Darryl Strawberry? What makes him such hot shit? What's he got that I don't got?"

GARY. Two hundred thousand dollars.

DANA *(shakes her head).* Sad to say, I didn't have the answers. All I knew was I loved to play baseball. *(She lapses into silence for a moment, paints.)*

MICHAEL. But that wasn't enough. *(She looks up at him.)* It wasn't. It wasn't enough.

BLACKOUT

SCENE THREE

The common room. MICHAEL has put a tie on and DANA is tying it.

MICHAEL. Family week.

DANA. Yeah.

MICHAEL. My parents love it. You can only talk when it's your turn, so they get to yell at me and I can't yell back. Last time my mom brought a prepared speech.

DANA *(finishes the tie)*. There you go. *(As Darryl.)* You look fly, Dude.

MICHAEL. You know, I don't think anybody says "fly" anymore. And I don't know about the "dude" thing either.

DANA. What about—I called somebody "bro" the other day, but then I thought it was racist. So I went back to "dude."

MICHAEL. Maybe "man"? I don't know. Darryl Strawberry's a soft-spoken guy, I don't think he says stuff like that.

DANA. But I've been saying "dude" all along. If I change mid-stride, it's going to seem weird, isn't it?

(DR. GILBERT enters around "change." MICHAEL sees her immediately.)

MICHAEL. Hi.

GILBERT. Hello.

DANA. Hi. Doc. *(Awkward pause.)* I was telling Michael here, that you have to run fast to the base, and not change your stride, because if you break your stride, you can miss the bag.

MICHAEL. And get tagged out.

DANA. Exacatackly.

MICHAEL *(gives her a look)*. Thank you, Mr. Strawberry, for that base-running tip.

DANA. No problem, kid.

MICHAEL. And I have to go see my family now. Wish me luck?

DANA. Yeah. Good luck, Dude. Man. Dudeman. *(MICHAEL covers his smile as he exits. To GILBERT.)* So what can I do you for, Doc?

GILBERT *(shakes her head at the stupidity of that whole exchange, then—).* I was planning an outing for the unit.

DANA. Can we go bowling again?

GILBERT. I was thinking since the weather's so nice, maybe we could do something outdoors. I noticed that Warren Park has batting cages. Did you know that?

DANA. Battin' cages.

GILBERT. Yes. Wouldn't that be fun? You could go out there and hit some balls?

DANA. Huh. Well, here's my problem with that. I'm afraid if I go to the batting cages, I might have a flashback. Like, post-traumatic shock syndrome?

GILBERT. Post-traumatic stress disorder?

DANA. 'Cause baseball wasn't all gettin' jiggy and swappin' spit. Whenever people found out I was drinkin', they turned on me. They started throwin' trash at my head and yellin' at me— *(Mockingly.)* "Daaaarrrrr-yl. Daaaaarrrrrr-yl." It hurt.

GILBERT. I thought people yelled appreciatively. "Darryl! Darryl!"

DANA. Only if I did something amazingly fly.

GILBERT. Like when you won the World Series?

DANA. Like that.

GILBERT. That must have been nice, everybody chanting your name.

DANA. I suppose.

GILBERT. How many people are in a ball park?

DANA *(shrugs)*. Fifty thousand?

GILBERT. Wow. *(Beat.)* I've never had that happen, you know, fifty thousand people yelling, "Gilbert! Gilbert!"

DANA. Not even at like a, psychiatrist's convention or something?

GILBERT. No. So? Batting cages?

DANA. Well, here's the real thing. Contractually? I'm not allowed to do shit like that because I could injure myself and be out for the season.

GILBERT. I just thought it might be fun. Baseball is a game, right? I assume parts of it must be fun. *(Small beat.)* Because I never hear about the fun parts. I only hear about how hard it is. Not about the trophies, or the chanting, or the stepping out of the dugout and tipping your hat—

DANA. That hardly ever happens.

GILBERT. But it does happen, right?

DANA. On occasion.

GILBERT *(beat)*. So I hear you've been painting.

DANA. I've been painting chickens.

GILBERT. Chickens?

DANA. Baseball-playing chickens.

GILBERT. Of course. *(Pulls a piece of paper out of her pocket.)* Speaking of painting, I thought you might find this interesting. It's about an artist. Her name is Dana Fielding. *(DANA draws back.)* It's a review of one of her shows.

DANA. Not interested.

GILBERT. It's a glowing review. Six, seven paragraphs about how amazing her paintings are. How "inventive" and "vibrant" and "stunning." It's the kind of review most people would kill for. There's only one sentence

that's not completely complimentary. At the very end…
"There are some weak spots—some less than meticulous
shading, a preponderance of reds… *(Small beat.)* "But
these are hardly worth mentioning when the work is as
impressive as this." *(Small beat.)*

DANA. If it's hardly worth mentioning, why bring it up?

GILBERT. How many people do you know who bat a
thousand?

DANA. Nobody. It's too hard. *(Small beat.)* You're hitting
a round ball—

GILBERT. With a round bat. You've told me.

DANA. The ball's going ninety miles—

GILBERT *(overlapping)*. Miles an hour, I know. Only one
in a million people can do it.

DANA. Damn straight.

GILBERT. And how many artists ever get a review like
this?

DANA. What are you getting at? *(Beat.)*

GILBERT. If I have one wish for you, it's that you could
learn to enjoy your success. *(Beat.)* What do you say we
work on that? *(DANA doesn't answer. Then quietly, like
a chanting crowd.)* "Darryl! Darryl! Darryl!"

BLACKOUT

SCENE FOUR

*The common room. DANA is talking to ERICA, who is
having a very hard time.*

ERICA. So then…does it come and go?

DANA. What?

ERICA. The Darryl Strawberry thing.

DANA. I don't get what you're askin'.

ERICA. Dr. Stanton says you need to be Darryl right now, but I thought you could be Dana with me.

DANA. Is this some sex thing? Like you gonna pay some ho to dress up like Little Bo Peep and whap you on the behind with her sheep stick? *(Beat.)*

ERICA. I hope you don't think you sound black, because you don't. *(Looks at her.)* Is it because of the fifty percent? Because that's industry standard and Rhonda only gives me ten. It's not like we're getting rich. Rhonda always says, you know, being a dealer is like being an ice salesman in an age of refrigerators.

DANA. You sell ice?

ERICA. No, I sell art!

DANA. Huh. You know, I've been paintin' some pictures.

ERICA *(worried)*. You have?

DANA. Just for fun.

ERICA. Good for you.

DANA. It is good for me. *(ERICA looks away.)* You know, some people who've looked at these things, they think they're pretty good.

ERICA. I'm sure they're great.

DANA. You don't sound sure.

ERICA. Well…isn't it kind of soon for you to be painting again?

DANA. I never painted before in my life. *(Beat.)* I could go get the damn things right now, let you see for yourself.

ERICA. That's all right.

DANA. But you haven't even seen them and you're actin' like they stink.

ERICA. I didn't say that.

DANA. Maybe you don't got no faith in me. Maybe you
think I can't paint for shit. *(Small beat.)*

ERICA. Get them if you want.

DANA. I will. They're right down the hall.

*(She exits. ERICA gets up like she's going to leave. MI-
CHAEL enters.)*

MICHAEL. Hi.

ERICA *(doesn't remember him)*. Hi.

MICHAEL. Erica, right? I'm Michael. We met when you
were here before.

ERICA. Oh right, right.

MICHAEL. Are you here to see Dana?

ERICA. Well, I was here to see Dana, but I'm seeing
Darryl.

MICHAEL. Oh it's okay. You can still talk to her as Dana.
You have to translate it out of the Baseball, but it's easy.
(Quiet.) She has to stay in character when she's out in
the open like this.

ERICA. Well does she have to enjoy it so much?

(DANA enters with a couple of covered canvases.)

DANA. Michael, my man.

MICHAEL *(to ERICA)*. Oh, have you seen these? They're
great.

DANA. She doesn't think so. She thinks they suck.

ERICA. I haven't even seen them.

DANA. My point exactly. *(She uncovers the canvases.)*

ERICA *(looks, beams)*. Oh my God. *(Laughs.)*

DANA. You don't have to laugh at 'em.

ERICA. No! It's a good laugh. Good laugh. *(Looks.)* They're *amazing*.

MICHAEL. Aren't they great?

ERICA. They're fantastic.

MICHAEL. I gave her the idea for the hat.

ERICA *(studying them)*. They're really...they could potentially be kitschy, you know? But they're not. They're different. I mean, stylistically I see you. The brushwork... but the tone and even the colors are so fresh.

DANA. So you like them.

ERICA. I love them.

MICHAEL. I do too.

ERICA. I think they're a huge step forward.

MICHAEL. I think they're sad.

ERICA *(not listening. Still looking)*. Rhonda should see these. These could sell. *(Looks at them again. Getting excited.)* I wonder...you know I wonder if she'd put them in the biennial. She hasn't put the catalog together yet. It's not too late. *(To MICHAEL.)* This is the gallery's chance to show off its artists, you know. The best of the best. *(To DANA.)* Even if you just had a couple of pieces, it'd be so great. For all us. To say to people, you know...I'm not beaten. You didn't beat me. *(Looks at the paintings.)* I may be down, but I'm not beaten. *(Beat. DANA looks at the paintings.)*

DANA. I feel proud of them.

ERICA. So I can show them to her?

DANA *(hesitates, then—)*. I don't know crap about art, but if you think somebody would pay me for the things, I definitely could use the dough. I only have so many days left in rehab. Even though I have millions of dollars I still have to have the insurance pay and they're startin' to make some phone calls.

MICHAEL. Really?

DANA. Yeah.

ERICA. Wait a minute. You signed them Darryl Strawberry.

DANA. Yeah.

ERICA. How am I going to explain that?

DANA. Something needs explaining?

ERICA. If you don't sign it—I don't know how I can say they're yours. They're so different. Or if I leave it—people will think it's very weird. They'll think you've gone off the deep end.

MICHAEL. She is in a mental hospital.

DANA. Tell them the truth. Say you met this brother named Darryl Strawberry at the hospital. And he had these paintings of these chickens. And you thought they rocked. So you said, "Put them in a show."

ERICA *(pause. Thinks)*. Like an outsider artist.

DANA. That's not a term I'm familiar with, but yeah, like that.

ERICA. You're some guy who thinks he's Darryl Strawberry. Because you're crazy. *(DANA looks at her.)* And brilliant.

DANA. I'm just having fun.

ERICA. That's what's so brilliant. *(DANA doesn't like this. ERICA doesn't notice. Looks at the paintings.)* God I'm so glad they're good.

BLACKOUT

SCENE FIVE

The occupational therapy room. DANA is painting; she's almost happy.

GARY enters and gets his sketchpad and pencil and takes them to the table. He doesn't draw though, he watches DANA for a moment, then speaks.

GARY. What are you so happy about?

DANA. Nothing. *(Beat. She works.)*

GARY. Where's the drunk?

DANA. Michael. He had a…setback. His family was here.

GARY. Family week. *(Opens his sketchpad.)* He'll be hitting the bottle in no time.

DANA. You don't know that.

GARY. Seriously, what are you so happy about?

DANA *(stops. Smiles).* Erica called me. They've already sold my paintings. A collector came into the gallery and bought them on the spot.

GARY. How 'bout that.

DANA. Erica wants me to paint more. She thinks Rhonda's going to put me in the biennial.

GARY. So the world loves you again.

DANA. Well. I don't know about that.

GARY. Sure it does. The world loves you again and everything's gravy. You're set.

DANA. I do feel somewhat vindicated. I have to admit. She said the buzz was terrific.

GARY. This Darryl Strawberry thing really freed you up, huh?

DANA. It's like…you always feel like you have to get out-side of your own head, to get ideas. But I never thought to actually get inside somebody else's. You know? But when I paint, I imagine I'm him and it's like, I see my-self doing all these wild things. Like everything's new and I can do anything. I'm diving for balls. Throwing the ball all the way to home plate.

GARY. You better not throw to home plate. You better throw to the cut-off man.

DANA. Whatever.

GARY. That's a bush-league throwing error, trying to get it home.

DANA. Whatever. I'm just saying I feel like I felt when I first started. And I don't even want to talk about it any-more because it's hard to get back to that place and I don't want to jinx it. *(She starts to work again. Beat.)*

GARY. You afraid it'll quit working?

DANA. No. I feel good. Dr. Gilbert says let yourself feel good. Enjoy your success.

GARY. Right. *(Beat.)* This ever happen before? Where you thought you had it licked, but then it didn't last?

DANA. No. *(Small beat. She can't stop herself, it's like she's talking to herself.)* I mean, it's a constant struggle. But the thing to focus on is the present and how I feel now. And not to worry that things will go bad. The thing to do is to not assume that I'll crash.

GARY. Why do you assume you'll crash?

DANA. Because. I crashed before. But that doesn't mean I'll crash again. Dr. Gilbert says maybe I won't crash at all, maybe I'll actually get better. You know. Happier.

GARY. You gotta change your world view.

DANA. Exactly.

GARY. And not make assumptions based on the past and what's always happened in the past.

DANA. Right. *(Beat.)*

GARY. Because this would be bad, you know, if this only worked for a while. Because what are you going to do? Every time you run out of ideas, try to kill yourself and go to a mental hospital and then pretend to be somebody you're not? That's not very practical.

DANA. This wasn't some trick.

GARY. Of course not. I'm not saying it was. I'm saying enjoy your success.

DANA. Then say that. And shut up.

GARY. Okay. *(Beat. DANA paints, GARY draws. Stops.)* Here's something though: when I hear people say, "You should enjoy your success," I always think what they're really saying is, the reason you don't know how to enjoy it, is you don't deserve it. Like, "If I had your success, I'd know what to do with it. Too bad it's wasted on you." You ever think that?

DANA. No.

GARY. Dr. Gilbert might not've known she was saying that—you know, consciously—but I bet in her sub-conscious, that's just what she was saying. "Give it to me. I'm the one who deserves it. And I'd know what to do with it."

DANA. Dr. Gilbert doesn't want to be an artist.

GARY. No, she wanted to be a dancer. Trained to be a professional dancer but didn't make it, so she went back to school and got her Ph.D. and here she is, sitting in her office talking to crazy people all day, but secretly in her head, doing pliés or some such shit in her little toe shoes.

DANA. How do you know that?

GARY. I haunt these halls.

DANA *(looks at him)*. You're so weird.

GARY. I've heard her talk about it. She tried out for a couple of dance companies in New York, and she didn't make it. Then she had a kid and you know, typical story. Shattered dreams and whatnot. So here you come in, the professional artist, and I'm sure she's thinking, "What the fuck are you complaining about? I wish I had your problems."

DANA. She's an accomplished psychiatrist.

GARY. No she's not. She's a wannabe. A wannabe dancer. Everybody's a wannabe something. But nobody has the guts to actually try and be whatever it is they want to be. Because they don't want to find out they stink. Usually, is the problem. So they come up with a million reasons not to even try. "It's all who you know." "Painting doesn't pay." "Playing the harp doesn't pay." "Nobody even reads poetry anymore." *(Small beat.)* Which is true, that last one. I've written some arresting poems on the subject of Kevin Bridges and nobody will publish the things. There's only one or two magazines that even accept submissions anymore. And forget about getting a collection published, it's just your small university presses and they only put out one or two volumes a year, tops. All the major imprints are owned by multinationals now and all they care about is the bottom line. They spend twenty million dollars on your John Grisham, or what have you, and then nothing's left for the rest of us.

DANA. That's not John Grisham's fault.

GARY. Sure it is.

DANA. He started somewhere too, you know.

GARY. Yeah yeah.

DANA. Why can't he be an inspiration? You know. "If I work hard enough, I could be John Grisham."

GARY. No way. You think that? That's your problem, right there. Nobody's looking at John Grisham thinking, "How inspiring." They're thinking, "Fuck you, buddy!"

DANA. Not everybody thinks that way.

GARY. Who are you kidding? Of course they do. That's what I'm saying. The only way the wannabes get through the day is by convincing themselves that it's impossible to get anywhere, that there's no point in trying. But then somebody like John Grisham comes along and does it, and they have to face the truth: It can be done. It just can't be done by them. *(Small beat. Turns it on her.)* And that makes the wannabes sick. It makes them wish you were dead. And that makes you wish you were dead. And that's why you shouldn't enjoy your success. Because the same people who gave you that success, are the ones who are giving you that death wish and you can't trust those losers. These are the same people who treated you like you had the plague whenever your career was in the toilet. The same people who flocked to your bedside whenever you tried to kill yourself.

DANA *(quiet)*. Nobody flocked to my bedside—

GARY *(overlapping)*. Of course they didn't! They were disappointed. They wanted you dead.

DANA. Why?

GARY. Because then they can say, "I am King!" Not her. Not the one who makes things. But Me! The one who breaks things. *(Looks at his drawing.)* I know I'm better than her and I'll prove it. I'll drive her to fucking distraction. *(Small beat. Picks up his pencil.)* That's the only way the wannabes can get a foot up. Is to make sure whoever's on top goes down. *(Closes in.)* And then they stomp you. Stomp you 'til your blood flows black. *(He goes back to his drawing, starts filling something in quickly, hard. DANA looks at him, afraid.)* Hey, look at me. I'm drawing your favorite. *(Looks up.)* Negative space.

END OF SCENE

SCENE SIX

Occupational therapy room a few days later. Several canvases are leaning against the table, facing upstage. DR. GILBERT is looking at them. DANA enters.

GILBERT. You know you're really talented. *(Beat.)*

DANA. Thanks.

GILBERT. Dr. Stanton wanted me to talk to you. Your insurance company keeps asking questions. Why, if you're MPD, don't we have you on commensurate medication? For example. Are we prepared to face charges of insurance fraud? Small things like that. *(Small beat.)* We need you to be Dana.

DANA. Who?

GILBERT. Please, let's not start that again. *(Sighs.)* You were right. You weren't ready to go home. But now you're painting again, you're showing again. The woman from your gallery comes around for meetings in the common room...

DANA. You mean that art lady?

GILBERT. Erica Lind, is her name. And she wouldn't be here if you weren't Dana Fielding. The successful artist. *(Small beat.)* So we'll continue to work together on an out-patient basis…

DANA. I don't want to go.

GILBERT. We've arranged your discharge for Monday. That gives you a day to make plans.

DANA. You can't put me back out on the streets.

GILBERT. Monday morning at nine.

DANA. People will buy me drugs. They will. Just to say they partied with Darryl Strawberry. Just to say they got fucked up with Darryl Strawberry, man…had a forty and a blunt. *(Beat. GILBERT regards her, waiting.)* I only painted these so I could stay here.

GILBERT. No you didn't. They're too good. *(Fixing to go.)* I'll have someone from admissions come by in the morning—

DANA. I hear you used to be a dancer.

GILBERT *(surprised)*. Yes?

DANA. Why'd you quit? *(Small beat, then she answers.)*

GILBERT. I wasn't good enough.

DANA. Oh.

GILBERT. But now I get to help people. Or try to, anyway. I hope I've helped you.

DANA. I guess you've helped me figure out ways not to kill myself. So. Congratulations. Success.

GILBERT *(quiet)*. It is success. *(Beat.)* All right. I'll see you tomorrow, Dana.

(DANA doesn't say anything. GILBERT exits. DANA looks at the paintings. Long pause. She's trying to decide what to do. ERICA enters, tentatively.)

ERICA. Hello?

DANA. Yeah?

ERICA *(sees the canvases and goes right to them)*. Oh look, you've done some more. This is good, this is really good. Shall we spread them out here? We'll make a little gallery. *(She starts putting them back out.)* The lighting's not too great but that's okay, Rhonda knows what she's looking at. *(They're out. She studies them, satisfied.)* Yes. *(Back to business.)* So the plan is, we wait until the biennial and then announce that "Darryl Strawberry" is Dana Fielding. It won't be a surprise though. People have been coming in to see the two we have and they know—they're too advanced for an outsider artist. And then anyone who knows your work guesses and that's that. Word spreads fast on our little planet. *(Small beat.)* And everyone's very happy, by the way, to know you're doing so well. Roy especially. He was so worried. *(Beat.)* So are you ready for Rhonda?

DANA. Sure.

ERICA. Are you going to be you, or are you going to be him?

DANA. I'm going to be me.

ERICA. Great. *(Looks at the canvases.)* Excellent.

(She leaves. DANA stares at the canvases, no expression. Then RHONDA and ERICA enter. RHONDA seems a little nervous.)

RHONDA. I told Erica, this is a first for me. *(Hugs DANA.)* Crappy studios, people's garages. I had one guy who painted in the bathroom even. But for you I'd come anywhere. You've lost weight. You look great.

DANA. Thanks.

RHONDA. I'm so sorry you've had to go through all this.

DANA. It was nothing I couldn't handle, I guess.

RHONDA. Listen, I know you, and I know how you push yourself, but just this once I hope you can appreciate this and just let yourself enjoy it. Enjoy your success. *(Awkward.)* So tell me you're feeling better. You're feeling better, aren't you?

DANA *(thinks)*. Yeah, you know. I got a lot of people who love me. I've got my friends. I got God. I got Charisse.

RHONDA. I don't know Charisse.

DANA. She's my wife. *(Beat.)*

ERICA. She's being Darryl.

RHONDA. I thought you said she was going to be Dana.

ERICA. It's okay. Just say what you would say, but say it to Darryl.

RHONDA. There's nobody around, I don't...

ERICA. Trust me, it's easier. *(Too loud.)* Darryl, Rhonda loved your paintings.

RHONDA *(also too loud)*. Yes. They were very nice. *(Small beat. Back to talking to DANA.)* I mean, they were inspired. I want you in the biennial. But before we announce anything I wanted to see what else you've been working on. I don't want a repeat of last time. I don't want to put any pressure on you to show something you're not ready to show.

DANA. No problem. I got four more and I'm gonna do four more after that.

RHONDA. Goodness. Let me look at them. *(Pleased.)* Oh, well these are terrific. Very consistent. *(Quickly.)* Not that they wouldn't be.

ERICA. And you think you'll have four more?

DANA. Yeah. I did the batter and left fielder last time. Now I'm workin' through the position players. Then I'm gonna do something different.

RHONDA *(pleased)*. Really?

DANA. Yeah. I'm thinkin' some scenes in the dugout. Like maybe the right fielder crouched at the dugout steps, waitin' to run out and start the game. That's like a moment of hope to me. When everything's new. Waiting to run out there and start the game.

RHONDA. I see. *(Small beat.)* And are you thinking about focusing only on the chickens? Or...?

DANA. Yeah, 'cause the way I see it, if chickens are playin' baseball then the whole world must be made up of chickens. There's chickens in the stands and chicken umps. Chicken hot-dog guys. There's a butt-load of chickens.

RHONDA. Right.

ERICA. It's very imaginative.

RHONDA. Yes. *(Small beat.)* I wonder though, if you want to think about other subjects. Not just chickens doing other things, but something besides chickens even.

DANA. Like, goats?

RHONDA. Or even...maybe not animals.

DANA. Nah. I like the chickens.

RHONDA. Then you paint the chickens. You paint whatever you want, of course. *(Beat.)*

DANA. But?

RHONDA. Nothing. It's just that with something figurative, like the chickens...well there is a shelf-life for that sort of thing. Usually. I mean, with the blue dog, for example. At first everybody loved the blue dog but then the blue dog was everywhere, he was even shilling vodka on the back cover of the *New Yorker* and pretty soon people were selling T-shirts with blue cows or blue monkeys. It became a joke. It's...predictable after a while. *(Small beat.)* And if you don't progress, then there's a danger that people might dismiss you. They'll even start to doubt their own judgment about your earlier work. Maybe it wasn't as great as they thought. Maybe it was all hype. *(Beat.)*

DANA. Are you saying you don't want to show my chickens?

RHONDA. No, I'm not saying that at all.

DANA. 'Cause I've got something to sell, and either you want it or you don't—

RHONDA. I want it.

DANA. Then save your lesson in "art for retards" for somebody else.

RHONDA *(looks at her)*. Pardon me?

DANA *(indicating ERICA)*. She says the other two sold like that— *(She snaps her fingers.)* Which means it's a seller's market, which means I can find somebody else to take 'em who doesn't talk shit to me. Hell, I could prob'ly skip the middle man and sell 'em myself.

ERICA. I would hardly call Rhonda Block a middle man.

DANA. I'm sorry, I'm new to this, but if she ain't a middle man, what is she?

RHONDA. I'm a gallerist.

DANA. A what?

RHONDA. A gallerist. And by investing in your work I give it a certain imprint.

DANA. You ever paint anything?

RHONDA. You know I haven't. You also know that collectors are clueless. If I didn't tell them what to buy—

ERICA. If we didn't put the right people in the room to-
    gether—

RHONDA. Then do you seriously think anyone would give
    a good goddamn about your chickens? *(Beat.)*

DANA. So you put people in the room together.

ERICA. Yes.

DANA *(to RHONDA, getting it)*. And you...you own the
    room!

ERICA. Dana.

DANA. But hang on, do you even own it? Or do you rent
    it? *(RHONDA doesn't answer.)* So you got your name
    on a lease and you put out some cheese puffs and a box
    of wine and all of a sudden—what?—that makes you a
    player? Well where I come from you ain't a player 'til
    you play. It doesn't matter how many butt monkeys you
    got kissin' your ass.

ERICA *(to RHONDA)*. She doesn't mean it. It's not her.

RHONDA. It is too her. It's so clearly her.

DANA I'm good because I'm good, not because you say
    I'm good. Okay? You could never do what I do. You'd
    get up to bat, and the whole damn park would go get a
    beer. They'd go get a snow cone and smoke a cigarette
    and then they'd go take a dump. Just so they wouldn't
    have to see your sorry ass make a fool of itself.

RHONDA. Okay, I know you're mentally ill—

DANA. Bonk! Inside fastball right to the head. You're
    lyin' on the ground, twitching around like a squashed
    cockroach. Everybody's laughin'. *(Calling out, like a
    heckler at the stadium.)* "You suck, Gallerist! Get off the
    field!" *(Waving an imaginary piece of paper.)* "But I
    have a lease!" *(As the heckler.)* "So what? You're
    stinkin' up the joint!" *(As the gallerist.)* "I still want half

your money!" *(As the heckler.)* "Then you're a fuckin' leech!"

RHONDA. Oh—fuck you! *(Heads out.)*

ERICA. What about the paintings?

RHONDA. Just—call me! *(She exits.)*

DANA *(yelling after her)*. But me? I get up there and... hush! You can hear a pin drop. 'Cause everybody knows. I know and the world knows...here comes the man. Here comes the man with the sweetest swing in baseball. *(Yells.)* You hear that Bloodsucker? That's me! *(Turns on ERICA.)* That's my history! That's what I made! *(Beat. ERICA looks at her, disgusted.)*

ERICA. Well I hope you're happy.

DANA. No you don't!

END OF SCENE

SCENE SEVEN

The Rhonda Block Gallery. This time "Biennial" is painted on the wall and underneath it is a list of names: Dana Fielding, Brian Lamont, Salvio Ramirez, Layla Walters, etc., etc.

DANA is standing in the corner again, but she seems happy. Too happy. She has that fixed smile of someone who is either receiving a lot of compliments, or is on medication.

ROY enters in his black leather jacket and hat.

ROY *(tentative)*. Dana?

DANA. Hi!

ROY. Hey. How are you?

DANA. Great! How are you?

ROY. Okay. I'm really glad to see you.

DANA. You too. *(Beat.)*

ROY. I hear from Erica that things are going really well.

DANA. They seem to be going really well, yes. *(Small beat.)*

ROY. Well I'm glad. I really like your paintings.

DANA. That's so nice.

ROY. It seems like you're enjoying yourself.

DANA. I am. Yes. *(She looks off, smiling.)*

ROY. You don't want to talk to me.

DANA. Not at all. I'm really happy you came. That was so sweet.

ROY. I wasn't being sweet, I just—I wanted to say hello, and for what it's worth, I'm sorry. *(DANA looks at him.)* I'm sorry—I shouldn't have left you alone.

DANA. Gosh. *(She actually looks frightened for a moment, like she has no idea what to say. Then she takes a breath and smiles. Cheery again.)* Oh well, that's the way those things go, isn't it?

ROY. I guess. *(He looks at her, puzzled.)* Are you okay?

DANA. Are you kidding me? I'm a hit!

ROY. Right. *(Beat.)* Well, so long I guess.

DANA. Okay. Bye.

(He walks off. DANA looks around, smiles again. RHONDA enters, briskly.)

RHONDA. Here's how I feel about it: We don't have to be friends. I have plenty of friends. You're an important

artist, it's good for me if I can show your paintings. I
hope you feel it's good for you to be here.

DANA. It's great!

RHONDA. Then I hope you won't run off with Erica without considering the impact it will have on your career.
You can set her up, yes, but the question is, what can
she do for you? Whereas I'm a proven entity—

DANA *(sees somebody. Waves across the room)*. Michael!
Over here! Come over here!

RHONDA *(sighs)*. Will you call me then, so we can continue this?

DANA. I have an idea. You call me.

RHONDA. Okay. Then. I will. I will call you. And now,
I'll go mingle.

(She exits. MICHAEL enters. They knock fists, old pros.)

DANA. Dude. You showed.

MICHAEL. It's packed.

DANA. My pictures sold before the thing even opened.

MICHAEL. No way.

DANA. And Erica found some old lady who'll pay me to
paint more chickens.

MICHAEL. Like a commission?

DANA. Exacatackly. A commission.

MICHAEL. That's great.

DANA. Yeah. How was the meeting?

MICHAEL. It kept me from drinking for three hours.

DANA. One day at a time, man.

MICHAEL. I know, I know.

DANA. You just gotta work the program.

MICHAEL. I'm working it.

DANA. I gotta tell you, the great thing about this Dana character is everybody thinks she's nuts. Nobody wants to talk to her. I can get rid of people in five seconds just by bein' nice.

MICHAEL. That's great.

DANA. I just do like I do with sportswriters. Smile, and bullshit. *(Small beat.)* I think the Leech might be right though. Maybe I should paint something besides chickens. I don't know what, though.

MICHAEL. You'll figure it out.

DANA *(looks around again)*. You know, I'm done with this. You wanta get some coffee?

MICHAEL. Sure.

DANA. Let me go find my jacket.

(DANA exits. ERICA enters, as if she's been waiting for DANA to leave.)

ERICA. Michael, right?

MICHAEL. Right.

ERICA. Right. I thought, maybe I could talk to you about Dana.

MICHAEL. What's up?

ERICA. Well, I wondered how you thought she was doing.

MICHAEL. Fine.

ERICA. She's not really talking to me. I mean she talks, but it's in this sort of super-enthusiastic cheerful, polite mode. But I'm worried about her and I was wondering, does she talk to you?

MICHAEL. Yeah.

ERICA. And you think she's okay.

MICHAEL. She's fine.

ERICA. Because she's really keeping me at a distance.

MICHAEL. She's probably feeling a little self-conscious. Everybody knows she tried to kill herself.

ERICA. But she's so cheerful.

MICHAEL. Do you want her to be depressed?

ERICA. I want her to be happy.

MICHAEL. Well…I think she's happy.

ERICA. Good then. That's all I wanted to know. *(Small beat.)* I just wondered though…you know it's always been our plan that when I started my own gallery, she'd come with me. But she hasn't said anything about it lately. I'm afraid she's going to stay with Rhonda.

MICHAEL. Look, I wouldn't worry about it. Dana needs you. *(Shrugs.)* And you get pragmatic after a while. You take your help where you can get it and your friends where you find them. How you find them. It's not like you can afford to be picky.

(DANA enters with a jacket, smiles at ERICA.)

DANA. Hi! Congratulations are due to you! *(To MICHAEL.)* She got me a commission.

MICHAEL. I heard.

DANA *(to ERICA)*. We're going to go get some coffee right now, but first I want to thank you for all your support. Thank you!

ERICA. So I'll draw up a contract for that commission?

DANA. Terrific! I look forward to it.

ERICA. If there's anything else, you know, just call me.

DANA. Will do!

MICHAEL. Bye. *(ERICA exits. They watch her leave.)* She thinks you're going to stay with Rhonda.

DANA. Hell, I'm a free agent. They can fight over me.

MICHAEL *(helps her on with her jacket)*. I had an idea, I don't know if it's helpful or not. I don't know anything about art or anything.

DANA. What's that?

MICHAEL. I was thinking, if you didn't want to paint the chickens anymore, there were all those other animals you used to paint. From your comic strip? The tern. Contemplative Tern. And the gnat, whatever the gnat was. And the Ghost Bison. That one really struck me. I thought something about him was so...I don't know. So touching and sad. I really liked him. I thought maybe you could paint him. Or his decimated herd. *(DANA stands there, staring at him blankly.)* I don't know. It was just an idea. *(DANA doesn't answer.)* But you probably don't want anybody telling you what to do. I'm sorry.

DANA. No, it's just, I'm afraid I don't know what you're talking about.

MICHAEL. Your comic strip. That you used to draw. When you were a kid. *(She stares at him again. Then she shakes her head.)*

DANA *(straight)*. I wasn't into comics when I was a kid. I played a lot of sports. *(Beat. MICHAEL looks at her. He sees no sign of DANA. Sad.)*

MICHAEL. Right. *(Small beat.)* I don't know what I was thinking. *(Pause. Takes a breath.)* So tonight was a home run. Art-show wise.

DANA. Oh yeah. Good night. Stepped up to the plate, waited for my pitch... *(She takes an imaginary swing, then clucks her tongue to mimic the sound of the bat hitting the ball.)* Hit the long ball. *(MICHAEL watches as the imaginary ball soars into the stands, stepping in with the voice of the announcer.)*

MICHAEL. Oh yes, ladies and gentlemen, it's going…it's going…it's gone! And the crowd goes wild. *(He makes the roaring sound of the crowd. DANA looks at him.)* The crowd's going wild. Let's see that home-run trot. *(DANA smiles, then lightly jogs in place, head down, miming trotting around the bases.)* "Darryl! Darryl! Darryl!" *(DANA stops as if finished with the game, looks at him.)* Come on, tip your cap. *(She hesitates.)* They love you. Tip your cap. *(She grins. Then she looks up into the imaginary stands, the imaginary lights, and tips her imaginary cap.)*

DANA *(still smiling, still looking up, still tipping her cap).* Fuckers.

BLACKOUT—END OF PLAY

DIRECTOR'S NOTES

DIRECTOR'S NOTES

DIRECTOR'S NOTES

DIRECTOR'S NOTES